# HM NAVAL BASE CLYDE

The *Empress*, seen off Row (Rhu). The ship was effectively a floating reform school that could cater for up to 400 boys. She was paid for by several leading Glasgow businessmen. Formerly the Royal Navy ship HMS *Revenge*, she returned to the loch 100 years later in a somewhat different guise.

# HM NAVAL BASE BASE CLYDE

## KEITH HALL

The History Press

First published 2012

The History Press
The Mill, Brimscombe Port
Stroud, Gloucestershire, GL5 2QG
www.thehistorypress.co.uk

British Library Cataloguing in Publication Data.
A catalogue record for this book is available from the British Library.

ISBN 978 0 7524 6480 0

Typesetting and origination by The History Press
Printed in Great Britain

# CONTENTS

# FOREWORDS

*Commodore Mike Wareham, Royal Navy*

*Naval Base Commander (Clyde)*

It gives me great pleasure to introduce this updated history of Her Majesty's Naval Base Clyde. I have often enjoyed referring to the first edition over the years; however, it is only now that I have been asked to provide a Foreword for the second edition that I appreciate I have been witnessing history being created during the course of my own career, one that has had me seen me serving here in four separate capacities over the last twenty-three years.

As the Naval Base Commander, I frequently make introductory presentations to a wide range of people and organisations. On occasion it seems right that they should open with a reference to the sinking of submarine HMS *K13* in the Gare Loch in January 1917 and continue on from there to illustrate the enduring connections that the Royal Navy has had with this area. They include the era of Military Port No.1 during the Second World War, the establishment of a small shore support presence in the late 1950s, later supplemented by the arrival of a succession of Submarine Depot Ships, leading up to the extraordinary civil engineering project that took place in the early 1960s in support of that exceptional achievement that was the Polaris Programme. Until now the recorded history has culminated with the redevelopment of the old ship-breaker's yard into the current Vanguard-class support facilities, yet another massive civil engineering project.

While a lot has changed over time, there have been some constants, the most consistent and strongest of which has been the way in which HMNB Clyde has provided unwavering support to the UK's Independent Nuclear Deterrent and, indeed, its policy of Continuous at Sea Deterrence (CASD) that stretches back to 1969.

I am delighted that Keith Hall has decided to update his original work to reflect many of the more recent changes, and those still to come, particularly our journey to becoming the Submarine Centre of Specialisation.

There is something for everyone in these pages, whether you are an historian, someone who has worked in the Base, or a member of the local community. It provides a fascinating and fitting tribute to piece of local and national maritime history.

*Floreat Clutha!*

## *Peter Merriman*

### *Director and General Manager, Babcock Marine (Clyde)*

Having personally been involved in HMNB Clyde since the mid-1980s, it has been fascinating to watch the physical and organisational changes. The previous edition of this book gave great insight into how the Base developed into where it was after the turn of the century. From an individual and company perspective, this edition adds the phase where Babcock Marine became the industry partner, delivering the outputs on behalf of the MoD and Royal Navy.

I, and Babcock Marine, hope to be around to review the next edition of Keith's excellent work.

# ACKNOWLEDGEMENTS

I am gratefully indebted to the following for their assistance and support in helping me compile this book: the Valiant Jetty Project Team, Defence Infrastructure Organisation (DIO), Jacobs UK, for permission to use their photographs; David McGowan for his amazing pictures of HMS *Astute* 'arriving' at Faslane for the first time; the Photographic Section HM Naval Base Clyde for allowing me, once again, to 'rummage' in their digital archives and make off with the contents; Lt Cdr K. Stockton and his team at the Northern Diving Group; Lt Cdr J. Bark from the Faslane Flotilla; Colin Evans from the Astute Training Building; Stuart Little from the NATO Rescue Submarine; Colin Miller, the Base Emergency Planning Officer; the Fleet Protection Group for helping me make sense of what is a totally alien world to a submariner; Steve Dunlop from the Naval Military Training Section; John Laird for the photographs of wild (and not so wild) life.

Special thanks go to Cdr M. Wooller, Flag Officer Scotland, Northern England and Northern Ireland's (FOSNNI) Chief of Staff and Cdr R. Ramsey from Flag Officer Sea Training (FOST), who certainly went 'above and beyond' in making sense of my almost fully formed version of what their organisations actually do. I must stress any mistakes in the book are due to my inattentiveness – the people involved couldn't have been more helpful and showed a remarkable degree of patience towards me and my endless questions.

I am particularly grateful to Commodore M. Wareham and Peter Merriman for writing the forewords to this book and Cdr James Leatherby for his help, advice and support.

My thanks to Karen Hall for proofreading the embryonic manuscript, and to Amy Rigg and her colleagues, Emily Locke and Marc Williams, at The History Press for making sense of it.

A small book of this type, essentially an overview, cannot hope to reflect or do justice to the effort, commitment and ability of all Base employees to ensure that it operates effectively and safely. Their contribution to the Base is immeasurable.

All money raised by the sale of this book is being donated to the Base's community fund. MoD photographs included in this work are used under the Open Government Licence v1.0.

# INTRODUCTION

The Royal Navy (RN) has had a connection with the Clyde area since the First World War. In 1940, the Ministry of War and Transport bought a site in Faslane which over the years would eventually evolve into HM Naval Base Clyde.

In 1963, the first nuclear-powered attack submarine, HMS *Dreadnought*, arrived and since then the Naval Base has been home to the UK's strategic nuclear deterrent with initially the four Polaris submarines and now the four Vanguard-class Trident missile-equipped submarines. In fact, since 1969 there hasn't been a single day without a submarine on deterrent patrol, all operating from the Clyde. It has been home to most classes of nuclear submarines and, as the T-class submarines arrive over the next few years, the Base will have hosted and supported all classes of nuclear submarines.

The Base also is home to the Navy's seven Sandown-class minesweepers that constitute the 1st Mine Counter Measures Squadron. The Base also provides a home for the Royal Marines Fleet Protection Group, the NATO Rescue Submarine, the Northern Diving Group and a host of supporting units and departments.

The Base's role is to provide shore facilities for general support, weapons handling and maintenance of nuclear-powered submarines, surface warships, fleet auxiliaries of the RN and its allies. HMNB Clyde is managed by Naval Base Commander (Clyde) (NBC(C)), who is responsible for the effective and efficient management of the Base and is accountable to Chief of Material (Fleet) for the delivery of this support to the Navy.

The areas directly or functionally under the command of NBC(C) are:

- The waters of the Clyde Dockyard Ports of the Gare Loch, Loch Long and Loch Goil.
- The naval establishment HMS *Neptune* and all facilities at Faslane on the Gare Loch. Faslane is the technical and administrative centre for HMNB Clyde and contains the majority of the authorised site.
- The Royal Naval Armaments Depot at Coulport on Loch Long. RNAD Coulport is a mainly civilian-managed establishment providing weapons support for submarines and essential services for nuclear submarines when berthed there.

- The Clyde Offsite Centre, Rhu (COSC). COSC facilitates a multi-agency strategic and tactical headquarters for response to a nuclear accident and is the headquarters of the MoD Emergency Monitoring Team.

Faced with the necessity of reducing the running costs of the Base by some £40 million per year over a ten-year period, while not degrading the support to the UK's submarine-launched nuclear deterrent, the government choose to use a civilian contractor to provide specified Base services. This initiative was part of a project that became known as the 'Warship Support Modernisation Initiative' (WSMI). Babcock won this contract and since 2002 has been responsible for delivering specified services to the site.

I spent, or more truthfully misspent, my plucky youth at Faslane and despite all the claims on the various recruiting posters I seem to have spent most of my naval life here. Obviously the painfully beautiful sunsets and the exotic foreign locales that were often mentioned in naval recruiting literature were not meant for this young boy from Yorkshire. Now in my dotage I'm still here, essentially doing the same things, but somewhat slower.

Hopefully this book will detail the large changes that have taken place in the Base over the years; on four occasions it has been the largest building site in the UK and now is the largest military establishment in Scotland. It is the biggest single-site employer in the country, with more than 6,000 military and civilian employees on the site, 1,658 of them Babcock employees. It is generally accepted that the Base contributes £270 million a year to the Scottish economy.

*Keith Hall*
*Tumbledown*
*Clynder*

# PART 1

On 1 October 1996, the Clyde Submarine Base was renamed HM Naval Base Clyde. The name change reflected the elevation of the Base to 2★ status, with Flag Officer Scotland, Northern England and Northern Ireland (FOSNNI) transferring his flag from Pitreavie to Faslane; the integration of HM Naval Base Clyde and the business area of the Director Supply North; and the arrival of several minor warships. But the Base's story started many years before.

At the outbreak of the Second World War, it was anticipated that Britain would be subjected to air raids by the German Air Force. In view of this, during 1936, a sub-committee of the Committee of Imperial Defence was formed and each of the country's principal ports had its own Emergency Committee. Their main aim was to maximise capacity in the remaining harbours, should one or more of the ports become inoperable due to enemy bombing. On 7 July 1940, Major General Riddel-Webster wrote a memo summarising the Army's position. It emphasised the need to increase military capacity in existing ports and create new berths. A meeting was held at the War Office on 12 July 1940, where it was decided to explore both these options. A group was formed with representatives from the military, Ministry of Shipping and the LMS Railway. In the course of their investigations they visited Barrow, Maryport, Ardrossan, Craigendoran, Gare Loch and Oban. The committee decided that only three options were worth further investigation:

1.  Oban, although at the three local sites selected there the quay length was limited.
2.  The eastern shore of Loch Ryan at Cairnryan, which would allow the necessary berths to be built and was near the deep-water channel. The railway system serving the area was limited, however, and a bulk of the traffic would have had to pass through Carlisle.
3.  The Gare Loch, a deep-water, sheltered enclosure with ample manoeuvring room. Two possible sites were considered at the northern end of the loch: Mambeg and Faslane Bay. Mambeg, on the western side of the loch, would be a difficult site to pile because of rock close to the shore. Rail access would also be difficult and because of lack of room at Mambeg, the marshalling yard would still need to be on the opposite shore, at Faslane.

The committee recommended that the military port be built at Faslane. The inability to pile at Mambeg and the time it would take to construct the railway track round the loch head contributed to making Faslane Bay the preferred option.

A meeting was called on 27 August 1940 to discuss the findings of the report. Most of the ministries were present at this meeting, although the Ministry of Labour did not attend and, for some time after, raised several objections to the proposed port. Minister of Labour Ernest Bevin did not like the idea of a port run by the military. Regardless of the minister's concerns, it was decided to start construction at both Faslane and Loch Ryan. Faslane was the preferred site: it would require the shortest line to connect it to the existing railway system, it was within the Clyde air defence area, and it was assumed that partial use could be made of the port while construction continued. It was estimated that the total cost of construction at the Faslane site would be between £1.25 million and £1.75 million.

During February 1941, some 1,000 men were engaged in the building at Faslane; during the same period at Loch Ryan there were only forty. In the spring of 1941, both Liverpool and Clydeside were heavily bombed. Authorisation was given to build three extra deep water berths, both at Faslane and Cairnryan, bringing both ports up to the six berths originally intended. The construction work at Faslane was progressing well, despite the lack of barges and tugs, and problems with dredging the 'narrows' at Rhu.

Despite optimistic claims by the Ministry of War Transport, the port was not in a position to appoint a superintendent (Colonel Bailey) until 6 April 1942, and it was not until mid-summer that it could deal with large cargo vessels. The port was officially opened by the Secretary of State for the Ministry of War Transport on 8 August 1942.

Faslane, by any standards, was a significant port. Its six berths were all capable of handling vessels of 33ft maximum draught. It was provided with capacious quays for lighters and had an impressive array of lifting equipment, numbering some thirty-six shore cranes and a 150-ton floating crane. A 35,000-ton battleship could be berthed and over 1,500 railway goods wagons could be accommodated in the sidings at Faslane Bay.

The Clyde Navigation Trust (CNT), which represented the interests of the existing Clyde ports, expressed concern over the military port on two counts: firstly, the Clyde ports had already invested large sums of money in extending their facilities to cope with the increase in war traffic; secondly, the military port posed a very real threat, once the war was over, as a rival. To alleviate these fears, the Regional Port Director wrote in January 1942 that:

> The port would only be operated by Service personnel.
> It would not be used for handling commercial cargos as long as commercial berths were available.

When the war was over, the port would not be sold or leased without consultation with the CNT.

This assurance was to cause problems on several occasions during the port's wartime career. For example, a deck cargo of aircraft and 2,339 bags of US Government mail were delayed when the military refused to unload them, and special indemnities had to be raised before this particular cargo could be dealt with.

As the war progressed, it became apparent that the Atlantic coast ports were not being subjected to the extent of enemy bombing that had been envisaged at the outbreak of the war. As a result Faslane had redundant capacity. With the preparations for Operation Overlord (the invasion of Europe) on the south coast and the vast amount of stores required, the War Office felt the skilled dock troops could be better deployed. In March 1943, Faslane (Military Port No.1) was manned by twenty-five HQ staff, 200 men on port maintenance, 150 in the wharfmasters' section, 180 on cargo securing and 200 operating the port railway. The government asked the railway companies to take over the running of the port railways, but the companies declined and left the War Department (WD) with little option other than to scale down its operations at the military ports. From February 1944, Cairnryan was put on a care and maintenance basis and the number of staff at Faslane greatly decreased. The requirement at Faslane was to retain the lighterage wharf, two deep-water berths and the 150-ton crane. It would also be needed for the troopship movements connected with Operation Overlord. The WD railway handled its first passenger train on 5 August 1943, when Winston Churchill embarked from the port for the USA. In March 1945, the War Office stated that Military Port No.1 (Faslane) would not be needed after the war had ended in Europe. Military Port No.2 (Cairnryan) could cope with the Army's needs for training and the war against Japan. Considerable pressure was put on the government to ensure that the promises made during the conflict about Faslane not being sold as a commercial port were kept. In April 1945, the War Office decided that the site should be leased to a ship-breaking firm. Although this decision pleased the CNT, it did not suit everyone. A firm of freight brokers, who had an office at Faslane, wanted to continue its operations, and the railway companies suggested Faslane would be a suitable location to undertake the now long-overdue wagon repairs, using prisoner-of-war labour. The discussion dragged on and the Army, against this background of uncertainty, announced that the port would close for all operations on 31 March 1946.

Tenders to lease the Faslane site were received from three ship-breaking firms; Metal Industries were clearly the favoured choice and during April 1946 discussions began in earnest with the company. On 22 July 1946, the firm sent the government an offer to lease the site and purchase the plant for £102,500. The offer was accepted and the company took over the lease from 31 July. The former military port was formally handed over to the Ministry of Transport Port and

Canal Directorate on 15 August 1946 and from the ministry to Metal Industries on the same day. This handover procedure was later to cause many problems when the government assessed an undervaluation of the site by some £100,000.

Most of the Royal Navy's capital ships were laid up in the Gare Loch in the mid-1950s. On 15 July 1956 some 200,000 tons of naval vessels were awaiting disposal in the loch. These included three battleships, two aircraft carriers and the cruiser *Swiftsure*. The majority of the workers at the Metal Industries Faslane site were Polish, displaced after the Second World War, and who lived on site in the former Army huts.

In 1954 a shore support building was constructed at Faslane for the experimental hydrogen peroxide-powered submarines. The building still exists today and is known as the Southern Utilities Building (SUB).

The Germans had been conducting experiments with closed cycle propulsion systems that were independent of the outside atmosphere as early as 1911. In 1940, following the successful trials of the hydrogen peroxide-powered V 80, a number of similarly powered submarines were built. The principle of the High Test Peroxide (HTP) system was a closed circuit turbine, powered by gas, independent of the external atmosphere. The gas was generated by the decomposition in water of concentrated hydrogen peroxide (perhydrol or ingolin); fuel consumption was high and the compound was dangerously unstable. During 1946, one of these submarines, *U-1407*, built by Blohm and Voss and launched in 1943, was scuttled at Cuxhaven. This was subsequently salvaged and commissioned into the Royal Navy as HMS *Meteorite*; the intention was to evaluate the Walther HTP turbine. Vickers was given the task of carrying out the evaluation and on the strength of their report, two submarines were ordered: these were the Ex-class HMS *Explorer* and HMS *Excalibur*. During this period, Professor Walther and his team were brought from Germany to advise Vickers Engineers at Barrow. These were purely experimental submarines, unarmed but impressively fast, with submerged speeds in excess of 25 knots. Perhaps not surprisingly, they experienced many teething troubles; in fact, HMS *Explorer*'s first captain never took her to sea. As mentioned earlier, HTP was an unpredictable fuel at best; there were several reports of explosions on board the submarines and on more than one occasion the crew had to 'abandon' ship and stand on the casing to escape the choking fumes that filled the submarine's interior. HTP was a very volatile substance, stowed external to the hull in special bags, which sometimes exploded while the submarine was underway. While the submarines were at sea, the engine room was normally unmanned, which was probably a sensible state, as it was not unusual to see fire balls 'dancing' along the tops of the combustion chambers. One member of the crew of a HTP boat remarked, 'I think the best thing we can do with peroxide is to try to get it adopted by potential enemies.'

On 9 September 1957, HMS *Adamant* and her flotilla of submarines left Rothesay to take part in a NATO exercise. On 12 October 1957 HMS *Adamant* returned from the exercise and entered the Gare Loch, accompanied by her squadron of submarines, two frigates and a floating dock, to establish the first British permanent submarine base in the loch. As the squadron grew, HMS *Ben Nevis* (a converted tank landing ship) joined the squadron to increase the availability of much-needed accommodation. As a depot ship, HMS *Adamant* travelled with her submarines, a luxury not afforded to HMS *Neptune* when she took over the role as 'depot ship' some years later. On 27 June 1958, HMS *Adamant* returned to Faslane after a visit to Bergen. HMS *Taciturn* and HMS *Truncheon* had accompanied her on the visit.

On 10 May 1958, HMS *Explorer* and HMS *Excalibur* joined the 3rd Submarine Squadron Faslane. During July of that year, the old floating dock, AFD 58, was sold to a Norwegian firm and removed from the loch. At this time the officers' mess was a thatched villa 'across the road' from the depot ship.

As the nuclear programme got under way, the HTP boats became redundant and were scrapped in 1969–70, eventually being broken up in Barrow.

HMS *Dreadnought* was launched by Her Majesty the Queen on Trafalgar Day, 21 October 1960, as a direct hybrid result of the 1958 agreement. The submarine's hull and front end were entirely British, and from the reactor aft to the main shaft was American.

HMS *Valiant* and HMS *Warspite* were the first all-British nuclear-powered submarines, although the reactor had many features of the American S5W reactor (S for Submarine; 5 for the generation of the design; W for Westinghouse, the designer), as fitted in HMS *Dreadnought*. The steam plant was entirely British and had been on trial on the Dounreay prototype for a number of years. Unlike the S5W, the British plant was optimised for noise reduction, and a considerable degree of success was achieved.

In 1952, Britain exploded its first nuclear weapon at Monte Bello. During this period a search a for suitable delivery system for the weapon continued. Between 1952 and 1968, Britain's nuclear deterrent was the responsibility of the RAF, carried as either free-fall or air-launched intermediate-range missiles. During the mid-1950s, Britain developed its own ballistic delivery system, known as the Blue Streak Project, but it was eventually cancelled. Work started on another system, Blue Water, but this again was cancelled in 1962. The cancellation of these programmes led to the decision to purchase an 'off the shelf' system from the US.

During 1955, the US National Security Committee decided to develop a submarine-launched ballistic missile (SLBM) system. Between 1955 and 1960, the Polaris missile was developed and by 1960, the first USN Polaris submarines were on patrol. On 10 July 1960, the first underwater launch of a Polaris missile from USS *George Washington* took place. Development work continued on the missile and by 1962, the A2 version was introduced. This, in turn, was replaced in 1964 by the A3. In its final stages of development, the Polaris A3 missile had a range of

2,500 miles and could deliver 3,200-kiloton warheads. The first test flight of the A3 took place at Cape Kennedy on 7 August 1962.

The first agreement between the US and Britain was for the purchase of the Sky Bolt ballistic missile under development in the US. However, in the early 1960s, the Americans cancelled the Sky Bolt project. On 10 April 1963, Harold Macmillan and John F. Kennedy signed the Nassau Agreement, allowing Britain to purchase the A3 missile system.

These missiles were to be housed in a British-designed and -built submarine. Early operating experience with HMS *Valiant* and HMS *Warspite* showed that, while the plant was quiet – a very desirable characteristic in a submarine, whose primary aim was to remain undetected – the reliability would have to be improved. The timescale for the Polaris programme was such that it allowed little or no time for extensive redesigning of the secondary plant. Commander John Warsop (later rear admiral), who died in 1995, was responsible for simplifying and upgrading the reliability of the secondary plant. The operating history of the Polaris Fleet paid a fitting tribute to the admiral's work. In fact, of all the features removed from the donor fleet submarine, or ship submersible nuclear (SSN), plant, only one was put back by subsequent alterations and additions action. HMS *Resolution* and HMS *Repulse* were built by Vickers Shipbuilding at Barrow-in-Furness. HMS *Renown* and HMS *Revenge* were built at Birkenhead by Cammell Laird.

It was decided that a shore facility should be built to support these submarines and their weapon systems. Several sites within the UK were investigated: Falmouth, Milford Haven and the Gare Loch. In the end, Faslane was chosen; the Firth of Clyde had ideal water for submarine exercises, sheltered but deep, with access to the open sea. Moreover, it is geographically neither too close to any town nor too remote. It is also readily accessible by sea, road and rail, and an associated armaments depot could be built nearby.

Development of the Base at Faslane commenced in March 1962. The depot ship HMS *Adamant* had moved to Faslane in 1958. The squadron was initially concerned with anti-submarine training and two frigates were attached to the squadron. The HTP boats were used for evaluation and training surface ships in tracking and attacking fast underwater targets.

HMS *Ben Nevis* (a converted tank landing ship) had been moved to Faslane on 10 August 1960 and was used as an accommodation ship for technicians and key workers involved in the Base's construction.

During January 1962, Metal Industries obtained a thirty-year lease on the land at the north end of the Base, and at this time, were the largest employers on the Gare Loch. HMS *Explorer* was decommissioned at Faslane on 5 March 1962.

On 24 May 1962, HMS *Maidstone* relieved HMS *Adamant* as depot ship to the 3rd Squadron at Faslane. HMS *Maidstone* had been refitted to enable her to support nuclear submarines. The first nuclear-powered submarine, HMS *Dreadnought*, joined the squadron in 1963. Tragedy struck the embryonic Base on 8 May 1963, when the Vista Club (NAAFI) burnt down. The club was originally opened in 1959.

On 21 May 1963, the government placed orders for the Polaris submarines and the major works began at Faslane a day later. Work started on the Polaris School on 3 January 1964. The school was opened on 30 June 1966, thus avoiding the need to send people to the United States to the USN Guided Missile School at Dam Neck, Virginia. Later in 1964, the Ministry of Works announced in June that the Armaments Depot for the Polaris submarines would be built at Coulport. On 10 July 1964, building started on the floating dock AFD 60 at Portsmouth Dockyard. A year later, on 4 October 1965, the A814 road diversion around the Base was opened. On 18 April 1966, the Central Reprographic Services opened for business in the Polaris School. This section can probably lay claim to being the most rehoused unit in the Base.

The year 1967 was full and busy for the Base. February saw the first captain of the 10th Submarine Squadron appointed, and by the end of March, the Base was commissioned. On 10 August 1967, the Base was officially commissioned, with the formal opening being held on 10 May 1968 by HM Queen Elizabeth. The Base was now officially known as the Clyde Submarine Base, HMS *Neptune*. HMS *Resolution* joined the 10th Squadron on 10 June 1967. Captain Kent moved ashore from HMS *Maidstone* and assumed the title commander, Clyde Submarine Base.

During this period, facilities were developed ashore to support the new Polaris submarines that would form the 10th Submarine Squadron (HMS *Renown*, HMS *Resolution*, HMS *Repulse* and HMS *Revenge*). When the Base was commissioned in 1967, the 3rd Submarine Squadron consisted of HMS *Dreadnought*, HMS *Valiant* and HMS *Warspite*. The three Churchill-class submarines joined shortly after (HMS *Conqueror*, HMS *Churchill* and HMS *Courageous*). The diesel-powered submarine HMS *Oracle* was also part of the 3rd Squadron.

HMS *Maidstone* finally left Faslane on 23 January 1968. Perhaps to make amends, the Services Cinema Corporation opened a temporary cinema at Faslane, just to the south of south gate, on 18 February 1968. AFD 60 undertook its first of over 600 dockings on 10 May 1968, while HMS *Otter* was the dock's first customer. The year 1968 also saw the beginning of the Polaris patrol. HMS *Resolution* sailed on 15 June that year, on what was the first of 229 deterrent patrols, and on the domestic front Provost Williamson opened the new Churchill Estate Community Centre, supermarket and Drumfork Club on 13 August 1968. On 22 May 1969, 730 houses were handed over to the MoD at the Churchill Estate. The Sportsdome was opened by Bobby McGregor on 18 March 1969, followed by the dry ski slope, which was completed on 26 March 1969.

The Base complement in June 1969 was 6,541, divided as follows:

| Service: | HMS *Neptune* | 1,215 |
| | 3rd Submarine Squadron | 1,234 |
| | 10th Submarine Squadron | 1,654 |
| Civilian: | Faslane | 964 |
| | Coulport | 822 |
| MoD Police: | Faslane | 78 |
| | Coulport | 87 |
| Engineering Services: | Faslane | 311 |
| | Coulport | 176 |

On 30 June 1969, the RAF formally handed over the responsibility for the nuclear deterrent to the Royal Navy.

The early 1970s were particularly unpleasant years for submariners. On 31 July 1970 the Tot was stopped, and when it appeared things could get no worse, Captain Sea and Shore Training (CSST) was formed on 10 October 1973. The only highlight in these dark years was on 15 July 1971, when SM brooches were first issued. The civilian canteen was opened on 10 May 1974.

On 2 June 1981, the MoD published its proposals for the Trident works development at Faslane and Coulport. On 12 September, the Faslane Fair was held in Churchill Square. Later in the year, on 10 October, the MoD repossessed the land leased by Metal Industries. The early 1980s also witnessed the end of the American Polaris programme. On 2 June 1982, the last missiles were offloaded from USS *Robert E. Lee*.

During May 1984, the MoD submitted plans to the local council for approval of the Base development. Gaining approval proved rather difficult and the plans were finally submitted to the Secretary of State for Scotland, George Younger. On 7 May 1985, approval for the MoD plans to develop Faslane to support the Vanguard-class submarines was finally granted.

On 10 September 1985, development of the northern area at Faslane and the Trident Facilities RNAD Coulport commenced. On 10 July 1987, a major works contract for the construction of the Shiplift, Finger Jetty, Northern Utilities Building (NUB) and associated infrastructure was awarded. Work began on the Shiplift on 24 August 1987 and it was handed over to the MoD on 12 July 1993. On 10 January 1988, the Trident Project Contract was awarded; the main contractor being Norwest Holst Scotland Limited.

To ease road congestion in the lochside villages during the redevelopment work, two bypass roads were built. On 17 January 1988 the Garelochhead bypass was opened, shortly followed by the Glen Fruin Haul Road, which was officially opened on 20 January 1988. The year 1988 also signalled the start of the Module Repair and Calibration Facility (MRCF) project, which commenced that September and is now known as Northern Calibration Facility (NCF). It was completed on 10 February 1990. The General Purpose Support Store (GPSS) was completed on 10 September 1988, and in what was turning out to be a busy year for the Base, the first Faslane Fair was held at Helensburgh pier car park on 25 June. A year later, on 15 February 1989, Phase 1 of the Trident Training Facility was completed. The completed facility was opened on 10 July 1990 by the then First Sea Lord, Admiral Sir Julian Oswald.

During May 1990, the refurbishment and upgrading of berths 1–6 was started. On 21 May, the modernisation of berths 1–4 commenced and by 10 October that year, the berths 5 and 6 modernisation programme was completed and the infilling of the lagoons behind the berths was finished.

On 21 May 1991, the Strategic Weapons Support Building (SWSB) was completed. It was followed a few weeks later by the General Services Building (GSB), which was handed over to the MoD on 21 July 1991. This building houses the Vanguard-class submarine's off crews and the Submarine Training Department.

During 1992, the new medical centre was opened (10 July) and the Finger Jetty was completed (4 September). The year also saw the NUB completed (7 October) and by 20 October 1992 the dredging work in Rhu narrows, which was required because of the increased size of the Vanguard-class submarines, was completed.

The MoD Police moved into their new headquarters on 22 March 1994. In 1967, the police operated from Cliffburn Cottage (now the site of the new senior rates' mess). By 1970 the CID were working from temporary accommodation opposite the EWSD building. The police dogs (or initially one black Labrador named 'Bohea') lived at the back of the middle gate.

On 10 June 1993, AFD 60 docked its 600th customer, and July saw the Nuclear Technical Department (NTD) works nearing completion. The Northern Development Area Trident Support Facilities were officially opened by Malcolm Rifkind, Secretary of State for Defence, on 19 August 1993.

On 1 October 1993 the 3rd and 10th Submarine Squadrons combined, to emerge as the 1st Submarine Squadron (SM1). The new captain SM1 was Captain McLees, who had been captain SM3.

The Base's complement on 1 July 1996 was:

| | |
|---|---|
| Service ashore/afloat | 4,000 |
| Civilian staff, Coulport | 1,900 |
| Contractors | 3,000 |

▲ The Gare Loch showing the original shoreline of Faslane Bay. West Shandon House can be seen to the right of the picture.

▲ Initially there were several large imposing houses on the site: this is Balernock House, which stood where the old wardroom tennis courts were.

▲ Belmore House, which was originally built in the 1830s by local fisherman Mr McFarlane as a small, two-storey house. It was later acquired by a Mr Honeyman, who remodelled the house into its present form. It is now the headquarters of the Faslane Flotilla.

▲ West Shandon House, originally built by Robert Napier, eminent shipbuilder and engineer.

▲ Building the military port in 1941.

◄ Colonel C.A. Bailey, the port superintendent, inspects the port in December 1942. He is accompanied by General Sir Bernard C.T. Paget KCB, DSO, MC.

⋏ Metal Industries take over the site.

⋏ An aerial view of the marshalling yard.

◄ ▼ ►  Various views of the port taken between 1942 and 1944.

⋀   HMS *Vanguard* at the breakers yard.

⋀   From the air, the southern end of the Base in the early 1960s.

▲ The hydrogen peroxide test jetty and support building (now the Southern Utilities Building).

▲ The southern end of the Base.

▲ Piling operations in preparation for the hydrogen peroxide 'test shop' and jetty.

◄ Rare photograph of HMS *Adamant* alongside at Faslane.

▼ The foundations of hydrogen peroxide 'test shop'.

▲ A view of the Southern Utilities Building and its approach road, in its former guise as the hydrogen peroxide test building.

▲ HMS *Meteorite*, the former *U-1407*, a German submarine salvaged at the end of the Second World War.

▲ The Base as it was in the late 1950s, complete with recreational ground towards the right of shot.

▲ HMS *Maidstone* at Faslane, having been refitted to enable her to support nuclear submarines. She 'took over' from HMS *Adamant* on 24 May 1962, and her first nuclear charge, HMS *Dreadnought*, joined the squadron in 1963.

➤ The Base in the mid-1960s. Note the extensive development since the earlier 1950s photograph.

▲ Construction of the buildings that would house the administration offices, mess and recreation blocks.

▲ HMS *Maidstone* departs from Faslane in January 1968.

➤ The accommodation ship HMS *Narvik* leaving Faslane on 22 March 1968.

◄ The accommodation blocks near completion, in April 1969.

◄ Taken in the late 1960s, an aerial view of the Base facing south.

▼ The Base nears completion.

▼ The Base as seen from across the loch in the early 1970s.

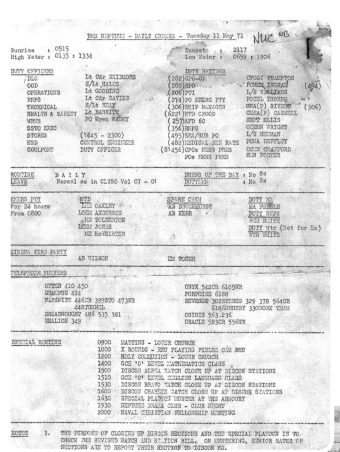

◄ A nostalgic look at Daily Orders from HMS *Neptune* in 1971.

► During September 1985 the building work started again, both at the Faslane site and Coulport, to enable the Base to support the Polaris successor Trident-carrying Vanguard-class submarines.

▲   The northern end development showing the Shiplift and the Finger Jetty.

▲   The 'small ships' of the 1st Mine Counter Measures Squadron.

# PART 2

## HM NAVAL BASE CLYDE

The Base's name and role change were the outcome of a series of reviews and studies undertaken by successive governments in an attempt to rationalise the Navy's role and 'harvest' the anticipated peace dividend at the end of the Cold War, while also managing to satisfy the ubiquitous, perpetual need to save money.

'Options for Change' was a restructuring of the British armed forces undertaken in 1990. It intended to cut defence spending following the end of the Cold War. Up to this point, UK military strategy had been almost entirely focused on defending the UK against the Soviet threat. With the collapse of the Soviet Union and Warsaw Pact it was argued that these scenarios were no longer relevant. While this rationale has been criticised at some length, it was a strategy adopted by successive governments of almost every major western military power.

Among the changes implemented were the cutting of services manpower by approximately 18 per cent to a total of about 255,000 (120,000 British Army; 60,000 Royal Navy; 75,000 Royal Air Force). Another major victim of Options for Change was the UK's combined nuclear civil defence organisation; the United Kingdom Warning and Monitoring Organisation and its field force, the Royal Observer Corps (a spare time volunteer branch of the RAF). Both of these organisations were run down and eventually disbanded between September 1991 and December 1995.

In the Royal Navy the number of frigates and destroyers was reduced from fifty to forty.

Several years later, 'Front Line First: The Defence Cost Study' was announced (14 July 1994) by the then Defence Secretary Malcolm Rifkind. Regardless of presentation, this was another series of cuts. Critics, such as the Labour defence spokesman Donald Anderson, argued that the cuts were driven by the Treasury. However, Rifkind argued that the front line of the armed forces was not affected and it was support staff and assets which were being cut. Rifkind stated that one of the major conclusions of the study was that the 'Ministry of Defence and other headquarters at all levels are too large, too top heavy and too bureaucratic'.

The main changes proposed in the study were:

- Closure of Rosyth Naval Base, although it would be retained as a Royal Naval Support Establishment.
- Reduction of MoD civil servants by 7 per cent (7,100).
- Further reduction of armed forces personnel by 5 per cent (11,600) in the following proportions: Royal Air Force – 7,500; Army – 2,200; Royal Navy – 1,900.
- These staff reductions were to include more than twenty senior military and civilian jobs at major general level and above.
- The closure of seventeen depots.
- The closure of two of the three military hospitals. It was proposed to set up military wings in several NHS hospitals.
- Army, Navy and Air Force headquarters to be merged into a joint HQ at Northwood.
- Several bases were to be closed; these were mainly RAF sites.
- To offset these cuts the study proposed two new major procurement projects:
  » A new class of nuclear submarine would be ordered: the Batch 2 Trafalgar class (these would become the Astute-class submarines).
  » The procurement of Tomahawk Cruise Missiles should be studied.

A few years after this, the 'Strategic Defence Review' (SDR) was produced by the Labour government that came into power in 1997. The Secretary of State for Defence, George Robertson, set out the initial defence policy of the new government, with a series of key decisions designed to enhance the United Kingdom's armed forces. Two of the largest defence procurement projects were excluded from this review: the Vanguard-class Trident submarines, which were replacing the ageing Polaris submarines, and the Eurofighter. The Trident system was essential to maintaining a credible nuclear deterrent – a policy adopted by Labour – and was already nearing completion. Similarly the Eurofighter was nearing production and its cancellation would lead to the loss of considerable investment and severe consequential penalties from the partner nations. The overall strategic conclusions of this review were that the British armed forces should be able to respond to a major international crisis which might require a military effort and combat operations of a similar scale and duration to Operation Granby during the Gulf War. It also should be able to undertake a more extended overseas deployment on a lesser scale (as in Bosnia) while retaining the ability to mount a second substantial deployment, which might involve a combat brigade and appropriate naval and air forces if this were made necessary by a second crisis (as in Operation Veritas in Afghanistan). It would not, however, expect both deployments to involve war fighting or to maintain them simultaneously for longer than six months. The armed forces must also retain the ability, at much longer notice, to rebuild a bigger (pre-Options for Change) force as part of NATO's collective defence, should a major strategic threat re-emerge.

To facilitate these aims, the Royal Navy's Fleet Air Arm was to merge their Sea Harrier force with the RAF's Harrier GR.7s to form 'Joint Force Harrier'. This joint force was to operate from Royal Navy Invincible-class aircraft carriers or air bases as required. The three Invincible-class aircraft carriers were to be replaced by two larger and more flexible aircraft carriers. These ships, the Queen Elizabeth class (known at the time of the review as CVF), were planned to enter service in 2012 and 2015.

To increase strategic transport, six Point-class sealift ships were ordered, and four C-17 Globemasters were leased. The SDR also reaffirmed the need for a permanent strategic transport force and the Airbus A400M was selected in 2000. Since that time, with operational tempo increasing, the seven-year C-17 lease has been extended.

The naval surface fleet force was reduced: from thirty-five to thirty-two frigates and destroyers, with the withdrawal of Batch 2 Type 22 frigates; from twenty-five to twenty-two minehunters; and the SSN attack submarine force was reduced from twelve to ten. The potency of the SSN force was increased by the decision to make all fleet submarines capable of firing the Tomahawk land-attack missile (TLAM). The SDR confirmed the purchase an initial batch of three Astute-class submarines.

The SDR stated that the maximum capacity of the Trident missile system would not be employed. Approximately 200 warheads would be maintained; this was a reduction of some 100 warheads. The SDR recommended acceleration of the retirement of the WE.177 tactical nuclear weapons.

After the 11 September 2001 attacks on New York and Washington, the Secretary of State for Defence Geoff Hoon announced that work would be undertaken on a new chapter to the Strategic Defence Review. This review would determine the UK's defence stance and planned to ensure that the country possessed the right capabilities and the right forces to meet the additional challenges faced after 9/11. The review concluded:

> We need to look further into how we should allocate the investment which is needed, including, for example, to intelligence gathering, network-centric capability (including enhanced strike and Special Forces capabilities and Unmanned aerial vehicles), improved mobility and fire power for more rapidly deployable lighter forces, temporary deployed accommodation for troops, and night operations. The significant additional resources made available to Defence in Spending Review 2002 will enable us to take this forward with the urgency that the 11 September demands.

It was against this 'far from static' background that the Base had to manage its business, and several initiatives were introduced in the 1990s in an attempt to satisfy constant demand to reduce costs. In the late 1990s, due to the decreasing naval strength, it became apparent that there was overcapacity in the surviving three naval shipyards (Devonport, Portsmouth and Faslane); this led to the Warship Support Modernisation Initiative, which essentially invited civilian companies to run the yards.

The company which won the contract to run HM Naval Base Clyde was Babcock Naval Services (BNS), which was a limited company, totally owned by the parent company, Babcock International Group (BIG). The original partnering agreement came into effect in September 2002 and saw BNS take over responsibility for the provision of engineering support, facilities management and other specialist support services to the MoD and Royal Navy, covering an initial five-year period through to August 2007. The £400 million, five-year contract was the first partnering agreement of its kind between the MoD and private industry. It was devised to deliver cost savings and improved service levels to the Royal Navy, and after the first two years it had proved a success on both fronts; BNS successfully reduced costs and improved service levels. This resulted in the MoD deciding to award an extension to the contract a year earlier than planned. The award of this extension to the contract brings the total value of the partnering agreement to approximately £825 million, increasing the savings to the taxpayer by £68 million.

At the time, Peter Rogers, Chief Executive of Babcock International Group plc, said, 'This early extension is testimony to the performance of the Babcock team and the strength of the partnering relationship with the MoD.'

Naval Base commander at HM Naval Base Clyde, Commodore Carolyn Stait, RN, added:

> We are now fully committed to our future relationship with Babcock Naval Services who have shown in the last two years just how efficient and cost effective a MoD/Commercial partnership can be. This produces real results for operational effectiveness and value for money for the taxpayer. I am genuinely excited about what this contract extension means for the Base and for our ability to support the fleet.

In March 2010, Babcock reached a long-term agreement with the MoD, guaranteeing work to 2025, and consequent savings of at least £1.8 billion.

• • •

The MoD's SLAM (Single Living Accommodation Modernisation) project was envisaged to provide all serving personnel with single cabin accommodation and to upgrade all shore-side living accommodation. The major building work started in 2003. The first major project was to rebuild the Base's living accommodation. This involved building eighteen new accommodation blocks, which would provide sufficient single, en suite cabins for the Base's 1,760 military personnel, including all officers and ratings. This significant task was further complicated by the fact that there was little extra space to build the new blocks, so the ship's company had to be shuffled around within the available accommodation while old blocks were demolished to make way for the new ones. The cost of this project was £125 million, and as well as the en suite facilities, each cabin had internet and television connections and some had amazing views.

The dining and recreational facilities were also rebuilt for the officers and junior rates. It was decided that these should be housed in one central block in order to save on galleys and other infrastructure. The resultant 'supermess' is a large, three-storey building that houses the wardroom and the junior rates' messes, dining rooms, bars and a central galley. This block also boasts a 'shopping mall' which contains a general store, coffee bar, bowling alley and barber's shop, plus a couple of other shops. The accommodation offices are also housed in this block, as are a number of lecture theatres. The senior rates' mess had been rebuilt a number of years earlier, although it now shares the galley in common with the other messes.

Another major undertaking during this period was the fleet submarine berthing project – the construction of a concrete floating jetty that would provide berthing facilities for the Astute-class submarines that were due to start arriving at the Base from 2009. This became known as the Valiant Jetty site at Inchgreen in Greenock. It measured 200m in length, 26m wide and 11m deep, and displaced a massive 44,000 tons. On completion, the jetty was towed across the Clyde and into the Gare Loch to be 'connected' to the shore-side works. A 200m-long roadway and three-storey jetty support building were also built by prime contractors Morgan Est and AMEC. The four piles that will hold the jetty in place are 70m long and 2.5m in diameter; each one weighs approximately 80 tons.

Once the work has been completed, all submarines operating from the Base will be stationed at the northern end, 'inside the floating security barrier'. This will reduce the authorised site footprint.

In June 2006, the Visitors Induction Centre was opened beside the Pass Office at the North Gate. The facility provides a computerised, site-specific health and safety, nuclear safety and security briefing, which concludes with a short multiple-choice exam.

The October 2006 Naval Base Review was one of many undertaken during this period – the review was intended to improve efficiency and effectiveness and to ensure that the minimum amount of funds were wasted.

In October 2007 Commodore Hockley replaced Commodore Stait as Naval Base commander.

The Base's Radioactive Effluent Disposal Facility (REDF) was refurbished during 2010. This was a major project designed to ensure that the plant would meet future environmental and radiological legislation.

Other major projects that were planned to transform the Base into the 'Submarine Centre of Specialisation' included the construction of a state-of-the-art firearms training facility and a new Incident and Command Control Centre. Other future projects include creating extra 'bed space' for some 500 military personnel, building new outdoor sports facilities and constructing new engineering and waterfront facilities.

HM Naval Base Clyde is the largest military, single-site employer in Scotland, employing over 6,000 people. It is a huge site, which covers Faslane, Coulport and the laid-up submarines at Rosyth.

# LODGER UNITS

## Flag Officer Scotland, Northern England and Northern Ireland

Flag Officer Scotland, Northern England and Northern Ireland (FOSNNI) ceased to have command responsibilities within Faslane when the Naval Base transferred to the Defence Logistics Organisation (DLO). Nevertheless, the nature and scale of the Royal Navy's presence in Scotland was considered sufficiently significant for the Navy Board to retain a flag officer north of the border. This decision was endorsed by the Secretary of State for Defence at Navy Command Transformation in 2006, and again in 2011 in the context of the post SDSR Navy Command Review.

The FOSNNI title now reflects the admiral's responsibility for engagement with the devolved administrations on behalf of the First Sea Lord, notably the Scottish Parliament, but also the Northern Ireland and Welsh Assemblies. This role complements his portfolio as Flag Officer Regional Forces (FORF), in which he is responsible for co-ordinating all aspects of RN engagement with civil authorities and society across the UK, outside the Base port areas. He is therefore responsible for: recruiting for the entire naval service (including the Royal Marines and Maritime Reserves); commanding the Royal Navy Reserve (RNR) and Royal Marine Reserve (as Flag Officer Reserves); supporting RN youth and cadet initiatives, including the Sea Cadets, Royal Marine Cadets, Combined Cadet Corps (RN) and MoD recognised Sea Scout units; the RN Presentation Team and he is also the admiral responsible for championing the Royal Marine Band Service and University Reserve Naval Units. These responsibilities are discharged on a day-to-day basis through the four naval regional commanders (Scotland & Northern Ireland, Northern England & the Isle of Man, Wales & West of England, Eastern England), who co-ordinate these activities with the visits to non-naval ports they facilitate for warships and wider civil society events such as Armed Forces Day. Through the naval regional commanders, FOSNNI is also responsible for the provision of maritime subject matter expertise at Police Gold HQs in the event of disruptive challenges such as floods and strikes. In the context of this role in the defence contribution to National Resilience, FOSNNI also commands operations to survey strategic ports and their access routes around the UK.

FOSNNI is the RN's Senior Security Risk Manager, in which capacity he is responsible for ensuring that the RN complies with MoD security policies and provision of direction and guidance to commanding officers, through the offices of the RN's Principal Security Advisor. This role also makes him the admiral responsible for the Royal Navy Police.

In summary, FOSNNI now commands some 4,000 personnel distributed across 100 sites throughout the UK. Yet by 2020, a quarter of the RN will be based in Scotland, so while FOSNNI could be considered simply to be a lodger in Faslane, in fact the Base is just one, albeit major, facet in FOSNNI's UK-wide responsibility to represent and explain the RN to the general public, a role that will only grow in importance as the RN footprint in Scotland grows.

## Faslane Flotilla

The addition of a 1★ post to the Faslane Flotilla reflects the increased size and scope of the Flotilla's role. The main task of the Commodore is to manage the Submarine Centre of Specialisation Programme. The ships and submarines of the Faslane Flotilla are expected to operate anywhere in the world in a variety of roles: from conducting major national and international operations as part of a task group, to independent patrols such as enforcing sanctions, intelligence gathering or providing humanitarian relief. Commodore Faslane Flotilla (COMFASFLOT) is answerable to the Commander-in-Chief Fleet (CINCFLEET) for ensuring that flotilla units can achieve these aims and that the required state of operational readiness and availability to enable operational deployment is maintained.

The flotilla comprises three squadrons of submarines and ships which are based and maintained at HMNB Clyde. The 1st Submarine Squadron (SM1), consists of the UK's Strategic Deterrent Force of four Vanguard-class submarines ('ships submersible ballistic nuclear', or SSBNs) and HMS *Astute*, the first of the Royal Navy's new class of SSNs, which arrived at HMNB Clyde in late 2009 and will be joined in the flotilla by her sister ships over the next few years. Over the coming years the Trafalgar-class submarines from Devonport will be joining the flotilla. The 1st Mine Counter Measures Squadron (MCM1) comprises seven Sandown-class mine warfare ships and a deployable MCM Battlestaff (including command and

▲ HMS *Astute* arriving at the Gare Loch for the first time.

▲ HMS *Astute* passing through Rhu narrows.

control facilities and engineering support). The Patrol Boat Squadron comprises two small five-man vessels, HMS *Dasher* and HMS *Pursuer*, whose primary role is the security of the Trident submarines.

The SSBN force is responsible for maintaining the UK's continuous at-sea deterrent. Three hundred and twenty-four patrols have been carried since 1968, with the average patrol lasting eight to nine weeks, and the longest, by HMS *Resolution*, lasting in excess of fifteen weeks. Not that the small ships of MCM1 are strangers to long deployments: on 25 November 2011 HMS *Bangor* returned to Faslane after 120 days at sea, thirty-seven of which were spent patrolling off the Libyan coast within range of Gaddafi's forces. She was clearing safe routes for merchant ships and carrying humanitarian aid. During the deployment she did not lose a single day due to mechanical or electrical fault.

With the forthcoming increase in the flotilla strength and the Base becoming the Submarine Centre of Specialisation, much work has been directed towards ensuring that facilities are available for submariners and their families in the local area. Flotilla staff have been liaising with local authorities regarding medical facilities, as well as the provision of housing and school places. Apart from all the UK's submarines being based at Faslane, all the support facilities, including all aspects of submarine training, will be centred at the Base.

## Flag Officer Sea Training (FOST)

Stationed in HM Naval Base Clyde, HM Naval Base Devonport, HMS *Raleigh*, HMS *Collingwood* and the Commando Training Centre Royal Marines in Lympstone, Flag Officer Sea Training provides the full range of training from individual tuition and unit level training to combined joint exercises such as Joint Warrior. However, the organisation is primarily recognised for its provision of Operational Sea Training (OST) to Royal Navy and international surface ships, submarines and auxiliaries.

Until 1973, sea-going operational training for submarines was carried out by staff from flag officer submarines. It then passed to the newly formed Captain Sea Shore Training (CSST). CSST was subsumed by FOST in 2001.

The shore submarine training facilities are divided between Clyde (Vanguard and Astute class) and Devonport (Trafalgar class). The facilities are regarded as world class and boast a variety of simulators including a control room trainer (warfare), a manoeuvring room trainer (nuclear propulsion), a weapons handling trainer and NUSCOT (ship control). NUSCOT is essentially the submarine equivalent of a flight simulator, where the teams can practise controlling the craft.

As part of the Astute Submarine Programme, some A-Class shore training was put out to a PFI and delivered by VT Flagship which, in June 2010, was acquired by the Babcock International Group after the establishment of the dedicated Astute Training Facility.

The Astute Training Facility's present shore facilities in the Clyde provide training for all personnel drafted to the Astute-class submarines. All their tuition takes place in a basic introductory ten-week course, which occurs in a specially designed twenty-seat classroom that allows computerised training and 3D walk-rounds of the submarine. Students can even 'fight' simulated fires and undertake extremely specialised technical courses. Despite all the high-tech training methods employed, all training staff are very aware of the submarine ethos, being ex-submarine crew, and students are encouraged to explore the branch history. The facility has a collection of submarine artefacts that are on par with the Submarine Museum.

All aspects of Astute-class training are undertaken within the facility and as safety regulations require ships' staff certificates to 'remain in date' these facilities are rarely quiet. There are also facilities for the ships' engineers to practise virtual repairs.

As the Base transitions towards designation as the Submarine Centre of Specialisation, the 'cradle to grave' training that will be provided by FOST will continue to be an integral part of submarine life. Learning from the lessons of the implementation of Astute training, the MoD, BAE, FOST and Babcock continue to look to the future to ensure the continuation of the world-leading training for the next generation of SSBN.

## Northern Diving Group

Clearance diving owes its name to the diving operations carried out by RN Port parties ('P Parties') at the end of the Second World War to clear the vast quantities of mines and debris that littered some European ports.

On 1 February 1996 the Scotland, Northern England and Northern Ireland Clearance Diving Group and the Clyde Submarine Base Clearance Diving Unit amalgamated to form the Northern Diving Group (NDG) at HM Naval Base Clyde.

The group consists of two teams (NDG 1 and NDG 2) which normally focus on different roles for planning and policy purposes, but are mutually supportive operationally. The group's area of responsibility extends north of a line drawn between the rivers Dee and Humber, extending out to sea, including Northern Ireland, the Orkneys and the Shetland Isles.

NDG 1 provides underwater engineering support for fleet units based at HM Naval Base Clyde, whether in the UK or abroad. The unit also provides support to visiting vessels, both UK- and foreign-based. NDG 2 is responsible for

▲ The 'bag' from a day's work.

▲ The team clearing ordnance at the Eskmeals live-firing range.

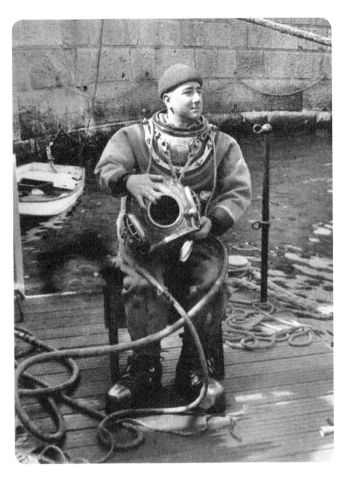

▲ All mod cons!

▲ Every year the team dive on the wreck of HMS *Royal Oak*, in part to check its material state. Here, team members are attending the memorial service with some of the ship's original crew.

▲ Lest we forget.

conventional munitions disposal and improvised device disposal in support of the Military Aid to the Civil Power policy (MACP) within the northern area.

Initially, outside the port the group operated from the Fleet Naval Diving Tender *Ironbridge* (that was for some reason known as 'Yo-Yo') and two smaller diving boats, *Emma* and *Jupiter*. During its first year of operation the group dealt with 247 operational tasks, co-operating with both police and coastguard authorities. In 2011, to the time of writing, the unit had responded to 104 call outs, including suspicious mail items, depth changes, unexploded shells and possible improvised explosive devices (IEDs).

## 43 Commando Fleet Protection Group Royal Marines

43 Commando Fleet Protection Group Royal Marines can trace its roots to the 2nd Battalion Royal Marines Light Infantry, which fought with distinction in the First World War, but was disbanded after the end of hostilities. Following the outbreak of war in September 1939 the decision was again made to raise a Royal Marine Brigade. As part of this brigade, 2nd Battalion Royal Marines was re-formed at Bisley on 1 April 1940. The battalion saw limited action in both Iceland and West Africa in the initial stages of the war, before the decision was made by Lord Mountbatten to convert RM battalions into commando units.

The 2nd Battalion RM ranks conducted commando training at Achnacarry in the summer of 1943 and 43 (Royal Marines) Commando officially stood up in July. The commando subsequently fought with distinction in both the Balkans and in Italy, which included the action at Lake Comacchio on 2–3 April 1945 during Operation Roast, at which Corporal Thomas Peck Hunter won the only Royal Marines Victoria Cross of the Second World War. At the end of January 1946 the commando was disbanded.

On 5 September 1961, 43 Commando Royal Marines was re-formed to create a fourth commando unit outside 3 Commando Brigade. The new commando resurrected the traditions of its wartime predecessor, including unit lanyard and flag, and the celebration of Comacchio Day annually on 2 April. The commando's second life was short and it saw no action in any of the post-colonial campaigns of its time, disbanding again on 15 November 1968.

In 1980 the growing terrorist threat led to the requirement for military protection of the booming North Sea oilfields and the newly procured Polaris nuclear deterrent, which resulted in the standing up of Comacchio Company at Royal Marines Condor on 1 May 1980. It was responsible for the protection of nuclear weapons, in static sites and in transit, and for the provision of reaction forces to counter terrorist incidents on offshore installations or ships at sea.

On 1 April 1982 the existing eight rifle troops were split into two companies, designated O and P Companies in keeping with the 43 Commando heritage. O Company was responsible for the Oilsafe operations, whilst P Company was responsible for the protection of the UK's strategic nuclear deterrent. An increase in size saw Comacchio Company became Comacchio Group on 1 November 1983, preserving the heritage and traditions of 43 Commando and the custody of the 43 Commando colours, which the unit still holds today.

On 28 July 1987 the Maritime Counter Terrorist elements of Comacchio Group were transferred to the Special Boat Service. The next major change occurred on 1 September 1992, when R Company was created to cope with the additional tasks being given to the unit. In March 2001 Comacchio Group RM was renamed Fleet Protection Group Royal Marines (FPGRM) to reflect the diversity of the group's activities and mark the relocation from RM Condor to HMNB Clyde. FPGRM now had a number of important responsibilities: Operations Sealion and Lifespan in Northern Ireland; security of the nuclear deterrent task force headquarters (CTF345) in Northwood; and an expanding requirement to deliver Royal Marines Boarding Teams (RMBTs) to ships of the fleet.

In April 2004 FPGRM expanded to over 500 personnel to provide resilience to the delivery of further expanding task list. P Squadron, responsible for delivery of RMBTs, was renamed S Squadron. In June 2010 P Squadron stood up again under the Fleet Protection Group, delivering Royal Navy force protection teams to ships of the fleet, as well as MoD-owned or chartered strategic shipping, which resulted in the unit growing to its current size of about 700. The creation of P Squadron brought, for the first time, Royal Naval ranks in large numbers into the unit, where, although not commando trained, they enjoy the ethos and traditions of a Royal Marines commando unit.

FPGRM, having recently been renamed 43 Commando, continues to preserve strong links with the traditions of the original 43 Commando, which are prevalent through the red and gold of the flag and lanyard, and the ownership of the 43 Commando colours, which are proudly displayed in the foyer of Gibraltar building.

In 2012, 43 Commando consists of three front-line Royal Marine squadrons (O, R and S) as well as P Squadron, comprising both RN and RNR personnel, to deliver the following operational outputs.

*P Squadron*

P Squadron delivers force protection to Royal Fleet Auxiliary Vessels, strategic roll-on roll-off vessels and mine counter-measure vessels (MCMVs). It is manned principally by Royal Navy junior rates, senior rates and officers, totalling approximately 165 personnel.

▲ Conventional combat training.

▲ Boarding operations training for the counter-piracy role.

◄   Vertical assault training.

▼   Close-quarters combat training in the skills house, Garelochhead training area.

➤   Training for boarding operations.

*O Squadron*

O Squadron provides the final line of security to the nuclear weapons based in HMNB Clyde and RNAD Coulport. Troops are held at very high readiness to achieve 'final denial' against any threat to the warheads, missiles or submarines that provide the nation's continuous at-sea nuclear deterrent.

*R Squadron*

R Squadron is responsible for the delivery of all dynamic nuclear movement operations, including a high-end close-quarters combat capability for static nuclear security and submarine surface transit escort.

*S Squadron*

S Squadron provides the RN with boarding teams in support of counter-piracy, counter-narcotics and anti-terrorism operations, and has reacted at short notice for evacuation operations, humanitarian relief, medical emergencies and force-protection duties worldwide.

## The NATO Submarine Rescue System (NSRS)

From the very earliest days of the submarine service, rescuing crews of marooned vessels has always been a prime concern. Unfortunately, unlike surface ships, submarines presented rescuers with a unique set of problems: crews couldn't, generally, be saved by lifeboat or simply by jumping overboard, like on a surface vessel, as there was every chance that the stranded submarine would be below the surface. These problems could be further compounded by such factors as the cold and the ambient atmospheric pressure. These issues have become even more significant as submarine technology advanced, operating depths increased and submarines roamed further afield.

First-generation rescue systems were based around a diving bell that was lowered to the stricken submarine and attempted to lock on to a hatch. The Americans were particularly enthusiastic about this method, having been stung into action by two submarine losses during the 1920s (*S-51* during September 1925 and *S-4* during December 1927). The latter incident had resulted in the loss of all crew members, despite the entire crew managing to reach a non-flooded compartment of the vessel. The tragic events of the *S-4* led Charles B. 'Swede' Momsen to propose a diving bell-type 'rescue' chamber. Several years later Lt Cdr Allan Rockwell McCann modified the chamber, and this improved version was used in 1939 to rescue thirty-three survivors from the USS *Squalus*.

Once submarines began to be used widely, it rapidly became apparent that the submarine crew would require a degree of self-reliance if their craft got into difficulties.

To this end submarines were fitted with various forms of escape equipment; the first of these was the Hall-Rees Submarine Escape Helmet. During the 1930s escape training was formalised and a specialised 15ft training tank was built at HMS *Dolphin*. At this time, escapees took up use of the Davis Submerged Escape Apparatus (DSEA), invented by Sir Robert Davis. Several years later, as a result of the Ruck Keene Report (1946) into submarine accidents, the Admiralty Board instructed that submarine escape equipment should be improved and that escape training should be enhanced. The most visible indication of this was the building of the 100ft escape training tank (SETT) at HMS *Dolphin*, which was commissioned in 1954.

Initially submarine escape, if the vessel couldn't surface or the crew abandon ship via more 'conventional' methods, involved flooding a compartment, waiting for the pressure to equalise, opening a hatch and 'floating' to the surface. This had to be done very quickly; obviously the submarine may be flooding but the overriding concern was to minimise the amount of time the escapees were placed under abnormal amounts of pressure. This was known as the compartment or rush escape. During the late 1950s the single-man escape tower was fitted to submarines, and although it only allowed one man at a time to escape, it reduced the time he was under pressure to an absolute minimum. On nuclear submarines two-man escape towers were fitted.

In 1949 the Royal Navy commissioned HMS *Reclaim*. Originally intended to be *Salverdant*, a King Salvor-class ocean salvage vessel, she was planned to be a deep-diving support and submarine rescue ship. She was fitted with underwater television cameras, advanced sonar and echo sounding equipment and a diving bell to assist in submarine rescues. In 1951 she was involved in the search for HMS *Affray* and one of her divers who helped locate the submarine, Lionel Crabb, was to find fame five years later while allegedly carrying out a covert reconnaissance dive on a Russian cruiser paying a visit to Portsmouth. 'Buster' Crabb never returned and despite rumours, conspiracy theories, numerous books and even reports of him being seen in Russia, the mystery of his disappearance has never been solved. HMS *Reclaim* also had the unusual honour of being the last British Navy ship to hoist sails; by jury-rigging a set of sails she could increase her speed to 12 knots.

During this period escape suits also evolved. Initially escapees were advised to wear as much clothing as possible in an attempt to 'keep out the cold'. Eventually, crews were supplied with immersion-type suits (particularly after the *Truculent* accident – see below). Once the escape towers were fitted, the suits could be 'plugged in' to an air supply in the tower. This inflated a life jacket, which in its turn vented into a transparent hood that allowed the escapee to breathe normally on their way to the surface. Before this, escapees had to breathe out all the way to the surface to ensure the expanding air in their lungs did not cause any damage. The suits became more sophisticated over time; the latest versions have a life raft stowed in the leg!

Since the end of the Second World War there have been as many as thirty-four submarine losses, four of which have involved British craft. All of these incidents

◄ Deploying the Submarine Rescue Vehicle (SRV).

➤ The SRV being launched from the mother ship.

◄ Recovery of the rescue vehicle.

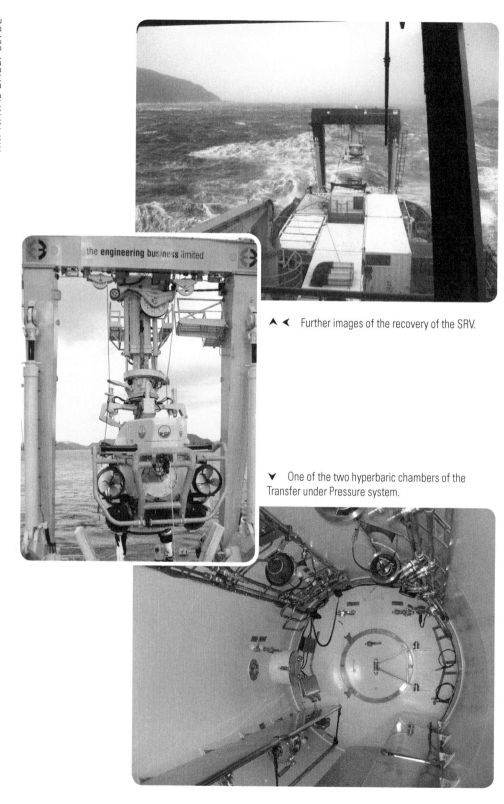

the **engineering business** limited

▲ ◄  Further images of the recovery of the SRV.

▼  One of the two hyperbaric chambers of the Transfer under Pressure system.

affected the submarine safety procedures, while some impacted on escape equipment as well:

### HMS Truculent *(1950)*

On 12 January 1950 HMS *Truculent* was on passage to Sheerness having completed trials after a refit at Chatham. In addition to her normal complement, she had eighteen dockyard workers on board. She was in collision with the Swedish tanker *Divina*. The submarine sank almost immediately and, although the majority of the crew escaped, many died of exposure, due to the harsh mid-winter conditions.

### HMS Affray *(1951)*

On 16 April 1951 HMS *Affray* sailed from her base port, HMS *Dolphin*, at 1600 hrs. She dived later that evening and was never heard from again. She had a crew numbering fifty men on board, all of whom were tragically lost.

### HMS Sidon *(1955)*

HMS *Sidon* was moored alongside the depot ship HMS *Maidstone* in Portland harbour. She was loading two torpedoes (code-named 'Fancy') when one exploded in its torpedo tube. The explosion was caused by the highly volatile fuel (hydrogen peroxide) that powered the torpedoes, but fortunately the warhead remained intact. (This is thought to be the same type of incident that caused the loss of the Russian submarine *Kursk* in 2000.) The explosion ruptured the tube the torpedo was loaded into, split the pressure hull and damaged the two furthest forward watertight bulkheads. Twelve men in the forward compartments died instantly and seven others were seriously injured. About half an hour after the initial explosion the submarine sank.

### HMS Artemis *(1971)*

On 1 July 1971 the submarine sank in 9m of water while moored alongside at HMS *Dolphin*. She was taking on fuel at the time and the stern dipped, allowing water to flood in through the open aft hatch. Although several personnel were initially trapped on board, all eventually managed to escape.

• • •

More recently, on 7 August 2005 a small Russian submarine became trapped in fishing nets 600ft below the surface of the sea off the east coast of Russia. Unlike the *Kursk* incident some years earlier, the Russians quickly requested international aid. The British rescue team reached the scene first, as the American team was held up in in San Diego due to problems loading their equipment on the cargo plane.

The British remotely operated vehicle (ROV), which was operated by Cable and Wireless and was based in Renfrew, was able to cut through the nets and free the

Russian submarine. All seven crew members of the 44ft vessel were rescued alive, making this one of the more successful rescue operations.

The most up-to-date incarnation of the submarine rescue system is the NSRS, a third-generation rescue system that is intended to rescue crews directly from their stricken submarine. It is jointly owned by France, Norway and the UK. There are essentially two parts to the system that can be either used together or independently. The smaller of the two is the 'Intervention' system, a remotely operated vehicle, known in this instance as an IROV, which can be mobilised swiftly to the scene of the accident, in order to access the submarine involved. It can also supply the submarine with life support supplies such as food, water, atmosphere control equipment and medical supplies. The second part of the system is the 'Rescue' system, which consists of a manned submersible. This is a Submarine Rescue Vehicle (SRV) which can dive to depths of up to 610m. Once it has located the stricken submarine, the SRV will position itself over one of the escape hatches and lock on. Even though the atmospheric pressure in the submarine may be much greater than the original pressure in the SRV, following pressure equalisation rescuees can be transferred to the rescue vehicle. A maximum of fifteen crew members can be transferred per trip. Once the SRV reaches the surface rescuees can be directly transferred to the Transfer under Pressure (TUP) system. As mentioned, the submarine crew may have been subjected to greater than normal atmospheric pressures for considerable periods; if, on reaching the surface, they were allowed to leave the SRV directly into normal atmospheric pressure they could suffer decompression sickness ('the bends'). Therefore, those who have been rescued are, if necessary, kept under pressure; transfer from the SRV to the TUP can take place whilst under pressure up to 6 bar (six times the regular atmospheric pressure).

This unit has two identical decompression chambers, capable of accommodating seventy-two rescued crew members and support staff. The 120-ton TUP also includes oxygen transport modules, a workshop and the environmental control cabin. There are also two portable two-man decompression chambers which allow the removal and treatment of individual patients, together with a medical attendant.

The Portable Launch and Recovery System (PLARS) is a transportable A-frame that can be 'attached' to the support ship to enable the SRV to be launched and recovered, safely, in conditions with wave heights up to 5m.

The entire system is capable of worldwide deployment and a fleet of twenty-nine trucks are kept on standby to move the NSRS to a port or airport. Staff at NSRS headquarters keep a track of all vessels capable of supporting the system.

The British, Norwegian and French navies provide overall command and control personnel. They also provide the necessary medical staff, TUP operators and divers/swimmers. Rolls-Royce provides the core rescue team that operates and manages the equipment. Various personnel, specialist in key areas such as ROV pilots and mobilisation assistance, are contracted in as required to support the core team.

◄  The team maintain a database of all ships capable of supporting the NSRS, and their current positions.

➤  Deploying and recovering the SRV.

◄  The SRV in action.

▲  The Transfer under Pressure system.

◄  The rescue vehicle undergoes an inspection.

▲ ▼ Launching the intervention ROV on calm seas.

▲ General view of Faslane Bay in January 2005. Work on the Astute Jetty has just started.

▲ The Astute Training Facility, where the Base now provides submarine training to all newly joined submariners.

▲   Apart from two sports halls, the Sportsdrome boasts a swimming pool, cardiovascular training facility, squash courts, tennis courts and a bevy of football pitches.

▲   Looking towards the loch in the west, across the area that is now the wardroom accommodation.

▲ ▼  General views of the site taken in 2005, across various buildings of multiple uses.

➤ The site's old accommodation blocks, seen in January 2005.

➤ The old and the new. This picture gives some idea of the space constraints the site's geography and requirement to keep working imposed on the building work.

▲   New accommodation blocks overlooking the loch.

▲   Looking north past the warrant officers' and senior rates' mess, the old 'mess and rec' block can be seen in the distance.

▲   Looking westwards over the site, the warrant officers' and senior rates' mess is to the left.

▲   The mess and rec block, seen in early January 2005, before demolition started in earnest.

▲ Demolition begins on the mess and rec block, 15 January 2005.

▲ Most of the mess and rec block had gone by the time this photograph was taken. Strangely, despite all the mayhem and demolition going on within the Base, the admin block (to the left of the picture) bravely soldiers on.

▲   Mess and rec block, 12 February 2005.

▲   The admin block, seemingly ignoring everything going on around it, April 2005.

▲ The mess and rec block, nearly gone, 30 April 2005.

▲ The demolition work continued throughout April 2005.

▲ ▼   The following pictures give some idea of the limited building space available on the site.

◄ Clearing the site for the wardroom sleeping quarters.

➤ An interesting view from high up, with the Sportsdrome to the right and the Shiplift in the distance.

◄ The admin block, still unfazed by all that goes on around it.

◄ ▼ These images from June 2005 give some idea of the rapid progress of the building work.

By June 2005, the mess and rec block had been totally demolished.

The former site of the mess and rec block, with the ever-present admin block behind.

▼ ▼ A series of photographs showing HMNB Clyde as very much a work in progress in June 2005.

▼ ▼ General images of the new buildings.

▼ ▼ These pictures taken in July 2006 emphasise the amount of work that had taken place.

▲   The Shiplift, with a very impressive backdrop.

▲   Looking to the south towards the loch in July 2007.

▲  The final blocks began to be demolished in July 2007.

▲  The digger gets really angry.

▼ ▼  Several views of the extensive building works in 2007, from across the loch.

▲ ▼ Construction of the 'supermess' got under way in September 2007.

▲ ▼   Further photographs of the site in September 2007.

▲ Wardroom accommodation being constructed.

▲   The supermess building work continues in May 2008.

▲   First wardroom accommodation being built in May 2008.

▲ Looking south in May 2008.

▲ Wardroom accommodation area.

▲ Amidst all this activity the admin block remains unmoved.

◄ ▼ Further shots of the supermess in May 2008.

▲   Entrance to the supermess – officers' and junior rates' messes.

▲   Entrance to the supermess shopping mall.

▲  Supermess from the west side.

▲  Accommodation blocks.

▲ The covered walkway from the accommodation blocks to the supermess – officers' and junior rates' mess entrance.

◄ One of the new single cabins …

➤ … and all en suite …

◄ … with a view to die for!

▲   Cutting up the old jetty deck.

▲   Removing the old jetty deck in December 2005.

▲ ▼  Removing the old jetty piles.

Commodore Carolyn Stait (third from right) looks on as the first concrete is poured

▲  Commodore Stait pouring the concrete base for the new jetty.

▲ The finished concrete base. The dock was used to refit the *QE2* a few years ago but it wasn't quite big enough, hence the 'dug out' bit, to fit the liner's bow, at the far end.

▲ The dock nearing completion, June 2008.

▲   The Valiant Jetty being floated out into the Clyde to start its short journey to the Base in May 2009.

▲   The jetty on its way up the Gare Loch.

➤ How the computer thought the completed jetty would look …

▼ … and how it actually looked.

▲ The site's chemistry laboratory.

▲  A view of one of the workshops.

▲  The Nucleonic Calibration Facility.

▲ Part of the active processing facility.

▲ The chippies' shop.

▲ The Base seen from the west side of the loch.

▲ A team from the Base's periscope workshop were asked to repair HMS *Conqueror*'s attack and search periscopes at the Submarine Museum, Gosport.

▲ The team were also asked to 'fix' the periscopes on HMS *Onyx* (on display at Barrow-in-Furness).

◄ HMS *Conqueror*'s periscopes in situ at the Submarine Museum; an improved viewing experience. The team have been approached to assist in the major overhaul of HMS *Alliance*, the display submarine at the museum.

➤ The Base is home to many wild animals. Here a swan and her cygnets have found a home on a pontoon in the southern basin.

▼ An S-class submarine leaving Faslane.

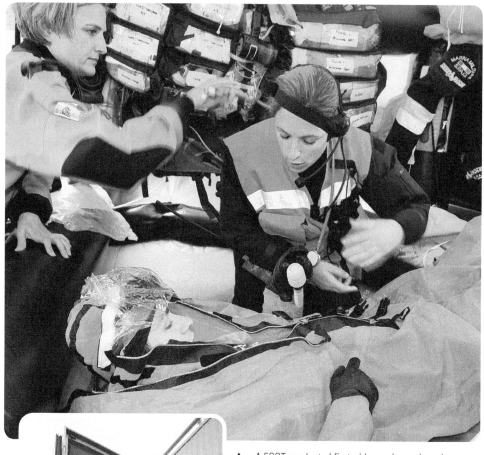

▲  A FOST-conducted first-aid exercise on board a minesweeper.

◄  The food arrives!

▲　Members of the Northern Diving Group prepare for work.

➤　HMS *Vanguard* escorted by a vessel from the Patrol Boat Squadron.

▲  HMS *Vanguard* in the Clyde.

▲  HMS *Vanguard* 'cold move': the reactor is shut down and the submarine moves under 'diesel electric' power, just like in the good old days.

▲ The Base's new shopping centre.

▲ The Mean Bean coffee shop.

⋏ Looking towards the entrance of the shopping centre.

⋏ The volunteer band.

▲  HMS *Ramsey* leaving the Base.

▲ The Brickwoods Field Gun competition started in 1907, after the Brickwoods Brewery donated a trophy to the Royal Navy. Unlike the Command Field Gun competition, which was held annually at Earls Court until 1999, there are no obstacles and the course is completely flat.

▲ The field crew in action.

▲ ▼ Time for a spot of relaxation in the bowling alley.

▲ Shopping for the essentials in the shopping centre.

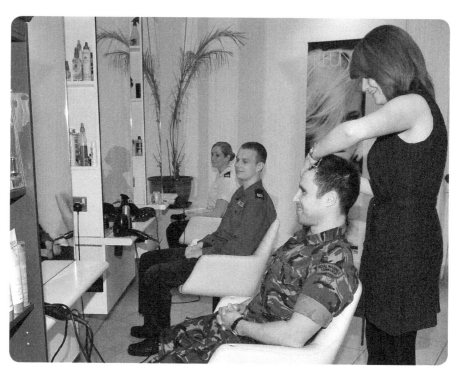

▲ The on-site hairdresser.

➤ Food, glorious food! At work in the food preparation area of the galley.

▼ HMS *Astute* leaving the Base.

▲  The swimming pool at the Sportsdrome.

▲  The Sportsdrome's cardiovascular suite.

▲   One of the Faslane flotilla returning to a typical Faslane welcome.

# EPILOGUE

What does the future hold for the Base? It would appear the prospects are good and its future is secure. At the moment the government seem committed to the Trident replacement; it will require a home well into the middle of the century. In the very near future the Base will be the only UK site with the ability to operate nuclear submarines and all the necessary support functions are being relocated to Faslane. At the moment the Base provides a quarter of the total jobs in West Dunbartonshire and generates over £200 million of income per year for the local economy. This can only increase as the Base grows into its new role; so as the Director and General Manager said in his foreword: 'I, and Babcock, hope to be around to review the next edition of Keith's excellent work.'

Whether or not I'll be around (or if I am, whether or not I'll be capable of writing it) I'm not sure; as I mentioned earlier I'm now fluttering around the upper branches of the chronological tree. That aside I'm sure the Base will provide the narrative for a book that will be well worth writing.

But in the interim I hope you enjoyed this book.

# APPENDIX 1

# HMCS *CHICOUTIMI*

Although the Royal Navy had decided that after the very successful diesel-electric submarines, the Oberon class, had been decommissioned they would be replaced with nuclear-powered submarines, it was felt that there was still a role for diesel-powered submarines. This was demonstrated by the activities of conventional submarines during the Falklands War, and diesel submarines could be built faster and cheaper than nuclear submarines.

Vickers Shipbuilding and Engineering Ltd developed the Upholder class from the 1970s onwards. The design was commissioned based on creating a 2,400-tonne submarine which had potential for export sales, while combining the lessons learnt from the Oberon class and the design of the Trafalgar-class fleet submarines. The submarines are packed with technology generally found only on nuclear-powered submarines, such developments including being built with teardrop hulls and having a fin built from glass fibre to keep weight down. The emphasis was placed on standardisation and automation to reduce staffing requirements. The first of the class (*Upholder*) was ordered in November 1983 and completed in 1990, and was followed by three boats (*Unseen, Ursula* and *Unicorn*) ordered in 1986 and completed between 1991 and 1993. Initially the Royal Navy had planned to order twelve boats, but this was cut first to ten and then to nine before being stopped at four. The rationale for taking this decision was the 'peace dividend' as the Cold War drew to a close in the early 1990s.

The submarines entered service from 1990–93. Initially they were based at HMS *Dolphin* (Gosport) but as they were so few submarines in the class it was deemed uneconomical and they transferred to Devonport Naval Base.

In their short period in service, the class operated mostly in the Atlantic Ocean, the Mediterranean and UK waters. The exception was *Unicorn*, which finished a six-month deployment east of Suez completing operations and exercises in the Mediterranean, the Gulf of Oman, the Indian Ocean and Persian Gulf. Her return in October 1994 to be decommissioned marked the end of service of this class, following a defence review by the UK Government that decided to maintain an entirely nuclear-powered submarine fleet rather than a mix of diesel and nuclear submarines.

In 1998, Canada accepted the four Upholders as replacements for their old Oberon-class submarines. After all four were obtained by the Canadian Navy, the

Canadian forces renamed them as the Victoria class. The first of the class, *Victoria*, was commissioned in Halifax in December 2000, with the further examples of the class commissioned as *Windsor* in June 2003, *Corner Brook* in March 2003, and *Chicoutimi* in September 2004.

Although the Canadian Government stated that the procurement was a bargain, there were arguments over the quality of the submarines and even suggestions that the purchase price of £244 million would have to be spent again putting things right. Canadian opposition parties demanded that the British Government fund any further costs, since it is widely believed that the submarines deteriorated while in storage and the Royal Navy was not completely forthcoming on their condition during the sale. It cost the Royal Navy £900 million to build the submarines and even if there were some minor problems, Stephen Saunders, editor of *Jane's Fighting Ships*, argued that 'there is not something inherently wrong with the class of submarines'.

On 5 October 2004 *Chicoutimi* sailed from HMNB Clyde to Nova Scotia. She declared an on-board emergency, north-west of Ireland, following a fire. The fire was caused by seawater entering through open hatches in rough seas. It soaked electrical insulation which had not been sufficiently waterproofed (as *Chicoutimi* conformed to an older specification than the three other submarines), starting a fire. *Chicoutimi* lost power and was rescued by Royal Navy frigates *Montrose* and *Marlborough* on 6 October. A Navy diver from the Northern Diving Group, operating from HMS *Montrose*, saved a Canadian seaman from drowning when he was washed overboard during the rescue operation. Diver G. Spence was subsequently given an Oak Leaf award.

Lt (N) Chris Saunders died subsequently from the effects of smoke inhalation; due to the rough weather it had not been possible to airlift him and the other casualties to a hospital until two days later. *Chicoutimi* was later transported to Halifax for repair. A Board of Inquiry cleared the captain of any fault but the regulations permitting the submarine to run on the surface with open hatches were revised.

Following claims made in the Canadian media about the cause of the fire, which essentially blamed the UK for supplying an unsafe vessel, the situation was further exacerbated by controversial comments made by Secretary of State for Defence Geoff Hoon. He accompanied his condolences for Saunders with a proposal that the Royal Navy would charge Canada for the cost of the rescue, while also stating that Canada as the buyer had to beware. In Canada, many Second World War veterans were outraged by his comments. However, despite all the media speculation, the accident was later proven to be due to an error in operational procedure.

# APPENDIX 2

# BABCOCK INTERNATIONAL GROUP (BIG)

In 1867 the Americans Stephen Wilcox and his associate George Herman Babcock patented the 'Babcock and Wilcox Non-Explosive Boiler' and a company (Babcock & Wilcox Company) was formed to produce these intriguingly named items. The company grew quickly, because as promised in the name, Babcock and Wilcox boilers had a tendency to remain intact, unlike most other boilers of this era. Two Babcock and Wilcox boilers provided the power for the world's first electrical power station at Holborn in London in 1882.

During 1891 they founded a company in Britain named Babcock & Wilcox Ltd which was responsible for sales outside America and Cuba, which remained the concern of the American company. Initially the UK company was based at Clydebank, near Glasgow, in the Singer Manufacturing Company's Kilbowie Works. The factory owner, Isaac Singer, of sewing machine fame, was a major shareholder in Babcock & Wilcox. During 1895 the company moved across the Clyde to a large 33-acre site near Renfrew, known as Porterfield Forge. Apart from large boilers for industrial sites the company produced smaller boilers for ships; it also made coal-carrying conveyor belts dock-side cranes and steamrollers. In the early years of the twentieth century the company was contracted to provide mooring masts and boilers for the Cardington Airship Base in Bedfordshire. It also built the mooring towers along the airship routes to Egypt, Montreal and Karachi.

Over the years the workload grew, particularly as a result of the two world wars, and by the 1960s the site covered more than 200 acres. During the Second World War approximately 10,000 workers were employed on the site not only producing boilers but also other equipment required for the war effort. The company manufactured tanks, shells, rockets and landing craft and even more esoteric apparatus such as fog dispersal machinery and steam catapults.

By the end of the Second World War the company had truly become a multinational concern, with offices in Mexico, Japan, Spain, Russia and Argentina. In the following years the company continued to move into new fields and grow. During the 1960s the company acquired Blaw Knox (makers of road-paving equipment), Gloucester Railway Carriage & Wagon Company, and Winget (manufacturers of heavy-duty construction machinery). The diversification continued with the company becoming involved in the building of pylons for the Generating Board; the maintenance of rail rolling stock; and the acquisitions of chemical engineers Woodhall Duckham, American Chain (suppliers of earth moving equipment), and Cable and Huwood Irvine (hydraulic machinery manufacturers). At this time the company became involved in the UK's nuclear power programme, building the 'two-legged' Goliath cranes used to build the new nuclear plants; two of these cranes were subsequently sold to the shipbuilders Harland & Wolff in Belfast.

By 1975 37,000 people were employed by Babcock worldwide, 22,000 of those in the UK. The company had offices, subsidiaries or associated companies in most parts of the world, and to reflect its worldwide reach the company changed its name to Babcock International in 1979. Three years later the company floated on the stock market and became a public limited company. In the same year, 1982, a Babcock-designed and built cradle was used to lift the *Mary Rose* from the Solent.

In 1987, in collaboration with Thorn EMI, the company won the contract to run Rosyth Dockyard. Babcock later went a step further and bought the yard when it was privatised in 1997, having already acquired the Thorn EMI share in 1994.

In 1995 Babcock sold its energy division to Mitsui. This was the start of a process to move away from manufacturing and concentrate on maintaining and supporting the critical equipment and infrastructure of customers. In 2002 Babcock was reclassified on the London Stock Exchange from Engineering to Support Services. In the same year the company was awarded the contract to run HMNB Clyde, and further acquisitions were made to enable the company to meet its aim of expanding into the maintenance and support fields. The purchases in those fields included: Huntington Defence Services (2001); SGI (2002); Peterhouse Group (2004); Devonport Dockyard (2007). On 22 April 2008 the company acquired Strachan & Henshaw, a major defence and nuclear contractor, from the Weir Group for £65 million. The following year the company acquired UKAEA Ltd from the United Kingdom Atomic Energy Authority (UKAEA). In 2010 Vosper Thornycroft (VT), the defence and services company, was acquired by the Babcock International Group.

On 25 July 2007 the British Government announced that the Aircraft Carrier Alliance, of which Babcock International is a part, would carry out final assembly of two new aircraft carriers for the Royal Navy at the Babcock-owned Rosyth Dockyard. Currently, Babcock is also the primary support provider to the Royal Navy; as well as being contracted to build the new aircraft carriers, it provides total support for the nuclear submarine programme and maintains three-quarters of the surface fleet.

Following Babcock's acquisition of VT, the company created four major divisions: Support Services, Defence & Security, Marine & Technology and International. It is now the leading engineering support services company, with an order book in excess of £12 billion and revenue c.£3 billion in 2010. Babcock